CORAL REEFS

CORAL

REEFS

FREDERICK WOODWARD

LONGMEADOW
PRESS

1 A featherstar (or crinoidea) on Marion Reef.

2 Exploring the Red Sea coral reefs of Ras Mohammed.

3 A Seychelles island, everyone's dream, with palm trees and tropical coral seas.

4 An irreplaceable golden treasure from Davy Jones' locker.

5 Coral reefs offer such sights to a privileged few but their survival should concern us all.

Acknowledgments
The author and publisher would like to thank Stephen Small, the editor, Design 23, the designers, and Suzanne O'Farrell, the picture researcher. The following individuals and agencies provided photographic material:

Bruce Coleman Ltd., pages: 1(Bill Wood), 11(Nancy Sefton), 12-13(Nancy Sefton), 14(Nancy Sefton), 15(Nancy Sefton), 16(Nancy Sefton), 17(Jon Kenfield), 51(Charles & Sandra Hood), 52(John Murray), 111(Michael Glover), 112-13(Fritz Prenzel), 114-15(Nicholas Devore), 120(Cliff Threadgold), 121(Barry Mayes), 122-3(David Austen), 127(Bill Wood)
Martin Edge, pages: 35, 37, 45, 55, 56, 59, 66, 77, 78, 117
Lifefile, pages: 40(Ron Williamson), 91(Sally Anne Fison), 92-3(Bob Harris), 94(Lionel Moss), 95(Richard Powers), 96-7(Sally Anne Fison), 124-5(Ron Williamson), 126(Emma Lee)
Linda Pitkin, pages: 2, 4, 5, 18-19, 22-3, 25, 28, 29, 30-1, 34, 36, 38, 39, 42-3, 48, 50, 53, 54, 57, 58, 60, 61, 62, 63, 65, 67, 68, 69, 70, 71, 72, 73, 74-5, 76, 80-1, 83, 100-1, 103, 110
Elizabeth Wood, pages: 3, 20, 21, 24, 26, 27, 32, 33, 41, 44, 47, 49, 64, 79, 84-5, 86, 87, 88, 89, 90, 99, 102, 104-5, 106, 107, 108, 109, 116, 118-9, 128

CONTENTS

INTRODUCTION 6

THE NATURE OF CORAL 10

LIFE ON THE REEF 46

CORAL REEFS AND MAN 82

INTO THE FUTURE 98

INTRODUCTION

At the present day in our modern, rapidly changing world, few habitats are more vulnerable than those of coral reefs, whose very mention conjures up pictures of warm, tropical seas, teeming with brightly colored fish, branching corals, and exquisite shells. In many ways coral reefs represent the forests of the sea, for they contain an abundance of marine animals and plants, which in turn demonstrate an enormous diversity in size, shape, color, and form.

The corals themselves, which are relatives of the solitary sea anemones of rock pools, also exhibit considerable variation of shape and color, even in a single species. This is due to variation in the surrounding environment, which influences growth and form through tidal action, water clarity, and food supply.

In addition, individual components of the reef community often display distinct interrelationships, some fish and molluscs being closely associated with particular coral species. The coral reef is one of the most fascinating elements of the complex natural jigsaw which forms the earth on which we live.

Man has been intrigued by corals throughout the ages and at first wrongly believed them to be plants because of their fixed sedentary life and brightly colored flower-like polyps. Their true position as animals was first shown by the English naturalist John Ellis in 1755, who studied living corals in west Florida and Dominica. He recorded his observations in his *History of Zoophytes* published, after his death, by Daniel Solander in 1786. This work included corals originally collected during Captain Cook's first voyage to Australia and the South Seas from 1768 to 1771. Several of these still exist to this day in William Hunter's Museum at Glasgow University and demonstrate the durability of corals as natural curiosities.

Cook's discovery of Australia and its coral reefs stimulated considerable speculation about their origin. Thus, in 1818, the French biologist and poet, von Chamisso, proposed that coral reefs and islands were formed by coral which grew to the surface and then stopped due to its inability to live out of seawater. He also suggested that the outer coral surface of the reef would continue to live and grow while the center would die and become eroded to form a central lagoon with its surrounding coral atoll. Then, in 1825, two Frenchmen, Quoy and Gaimard, suggested that reef-building corals inhabiting shallow water on the edges of a sunken volcano could also explain how coral atolls came into being.

Charles Darwin observed several offshore coral reefs during his voyages on HMS *Beagle* (1831–1836). He concluded that they began as shallow water fringing reefs mirroring the outline of the adjacent coastline, which, following earth movements and subsequent submergence of the coastline, then sank into deeper water. He argued that providing the subsidence was gradual, it would be feasible for the coral growth to keep pace, resulting in the formation of offshore reefs.

Later, Sir John Murray, the chief biologist on HMS *Challenger* during her 1874–1876 voyage, thought that corals may settle to grow on the elevated summits of submarine ridges, which, due to sedimentation from surface debris, were within the depth limits for coral growth. Recent evidence from drilling operations during oil exploration indicates that, although the seabed is slowly subsiding, it is probable that all of the above theories have contributed to coral reef formations.

All of the world's present day coral reefs are to be found in moderately shallow water. Some, however, are hundreds of feet thick as a result of the ocean floor sinking, or the water level rising, at approximately the same rate as the corals have built their way up toward the surface.

Since coral growth varies from five to 200 centimetres a year, depending on temperature, water clarity, and food supply, it has been estimated that some of the older reefs may have taken from 10,000 to 30,000 years to reach their present size.

Modern coral reefs can be subdivided into four basic types: fringing reefs, barrier reefs, atolls, and patch reefs. Fringing reefs normally occur in shallow waters about half a mile offshore, stretching as a narrow ridge or barrier parallel to the shore from which they are separated by still-water lagoons. These reefs are relatively young, the living coral being particularly abundant on the outer seaward surfaces of the reef.

Barrier reefs also lie more or less parallel to the shore but tend to be more mature. They are normally situated up to four miles offshore and often have small islands, fringing reefs, and patch reefs present in the area between this outer barrier reef and the mainland.

Atolls occur in deeper water. They are normally circular in outline and usually develop on the sunken rims of former volcanic peaks. The last type, patch reefs, occur as flat-topped reefs with sloping sides and normally develop on flat-topped elevations of the seafloor. They grow in both deep and shallow water at depths from as little as five feet. It should be emphasized that individual reefs often combine more than one of these four reef types.

Corals, and the reefs produced from their calcareous skeletons, extend back in time well before man's appearance here on earth. Indeed, remains of their early ancestors contribute considerably to the fossil record of the Cambrian, Silurian, and Carboniferous periods of earth history, which took place over 500 million years ago.

Because modern corals are all marine and normally occur in tropical seas, it is assumed that the seas of these former geological periods enjoyed similar conditions of climate and temperature. The concept that corals only occur in tropical seas is not absolutely true, however, since some modern corals live in colder climes, such as the littoral solitary cup-corals (*Caryophyllia*) and the deeper-water branching corals (*Lophelia*) of European seas.

The majority of corals, however, do not survive for any length of time at temperatures less than 68 degrees Fahrenheit (20° C), which explains why their chief distribution is in tropical waters. This may be due to the symbiotically associated algae present in their tissues, for these require light and heat in order to convert carbon dioxide and water into the useful food substances which are subsequently used by their coral hosts.

The corals concerned tend to inhabit relatively shallow water which will allow sunlight to reach them. In most cases corals also require crystal clear water without suspended sediments, since this not only prevents light penetration but may prevent active coral growth due to accumulating sedimentation.

Other species, such as *Lophelia*, which forms coral "reefs" off northeast Scotland and Ireland, and *Denrophelia* from the Mediterranean which grows up to two feet high, can tolerate cooler water. These feed purely on suspended organic debris and can exist at deeper levels since light is not necessary for their survival.

Coral reefs and their associated land masses afford not only a suitable place in which to live but also provide an important supply of food to human communities through the fish and other organisms caught in the waters around them. This is of considerable significance as coral reefs and their environs account for about a fifth of all seafood production. When one also considers the fact that about 60 percent of the world's human population lives within 40 miles of the coast, the utility of coral reefs for man becomes obvious.

It should also be noted that coral reefs, together with the mangrove swamps and coastal wetlands of low-lying coastal shorelines, have a protective function against violent ocean storms. They act as a barrier which greatly reduces the force and intensity of wave action by absorbing the enormous energy produced by the open sea during storms and hurricanes.

Unfortunately, these same coral reefs are being increasingly downgraded and destroyed by pollution and unregulated exploitation. Such destruction is of particular concern considering the increasing threat to low-lying regions posed by the rise in sea level that may accompany global warming. If only for this reason it is beyond question that urgent attention should be given to the protection of coral reefs.

Since World War II, humans have discovered more about the underwater environment than was once dreamed possible through the development of sub-aqua equipment. This enables us to observe completely aquatic organisms in their natural habitat, in both shallow coastal waters and the deepest ocean depths. The resultant awareness has drawn our attention to the serious decline in the quality of this previously inaccessible environment. We must now build on this awareness to protect the fragile world of the coral reef before these valuable and beautiful resources are irreparably damaged.

THE NATURE OF CORAL

What exactly are corals? These beautiful marine invertebrates are among the most primitive of multicellular animals (ie. animals made up of more than one cell) and possess a simple nerve network and digestive system. They belong to a group of animals, the coelenterates, which includes sea firs, jellyfish, sea fans, soft corals, anemones, and true corals.

Unlike jellyfish, corals and their nearest relatives have developed the polyp stage to the exclusion of a free-swimming stage, spending most of their life permanently fixed to the seafloor. The sea anemones consist of solitary polyps and, although devoid of a calcareous or horny skeleton, may reach up to two feet in diameter. Sea pens and sea fans have a horny skeleton, which gives them a passing resemblance to true coral, however, the skeleton of coral is calcareous rather than horny.

The calcareous coral skeleton consists of calcium carbonate crystals which are extracted from the sea and laid down by the epithelial cells of the base and lower body wall of the coral animal, which is known as a polyp. The coral polyp is thus protected by the surrounding exoskeleton (outer skeleton), into which it withdraws when danger approaches.

Solitary corals consist of a single polyp encased within its calcareous skeleton and are usually relatively small in size, but some, such as the mushroom corals (*Fungia*) have a large solitary polyp lying free on the seabed. Some of these individual polyps reach over eight inches across. The individual coral polyps of colonial corals are joined together by their epidermal cells, which cover the surface of the coral skeleton, and also by the interconnection of their digestive and circulation systems which are continuous between polyps.

Living corals exhibit a wide range of colors from creamy white, through reds, greens, browns to black, but once the polyps die these brilliant hues are soon lost. One notable exception to this is the red organ pipe coral, *Tubipora musica*, so named due to its skeleton being in the form of connected vertically parallel tubes.

Although carnivorous, many corals have associated single-celled plants present in their tissues and, since these plants require light in order to convert carbon dioxide and water into food, the corals concerned are restricted to relatively shallow water. These corals and plants are both capable of living independently of each other, but their association is so mutually beneficial that they are seldom found apart.

To imagine a world without these brightly colored creatures with their exquisite shapes and patterns is beyond contemplation.

11 A vertical Caribbean reef wall makes an
ideal base for mother nature's jigsaw of hard
corals and sponges, through which mixed
shoals of fish dart, sparkling like jewels.

12-13 A large colonial brain coral forms a
backdrop to several sea fans and a large red
branching sponge.

14 The brilliant purplish hues of this living
South Pacific staghorn coral are due to the
animal's pigmentation. On its death they are
replaced by the familiar bleached white
skeleton.

15 A portion of coral reef displays a variety of
marine life which has developed over several
centuries.

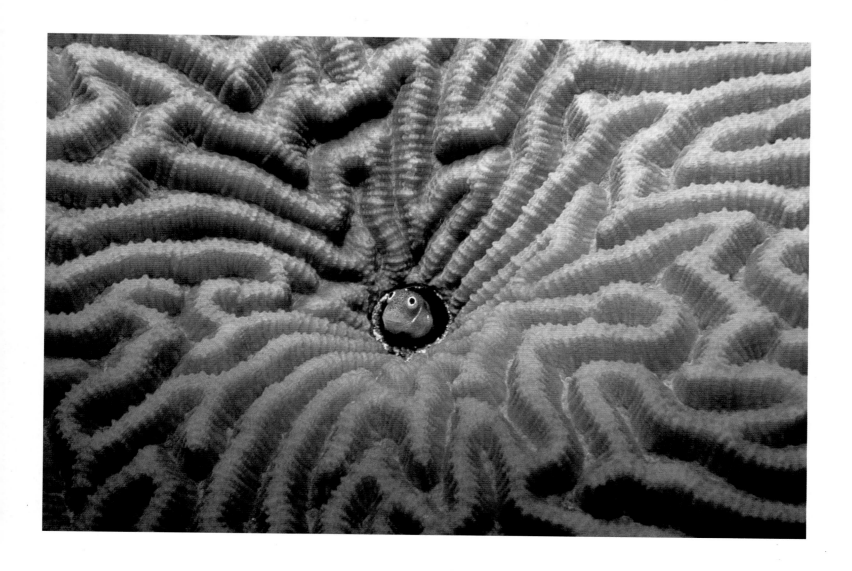

16 This soft sea whip coral from the Caribbean rises majestically above the general reef corals and sponges. Sadly it is much prized by divers which has resulted in its decline through over-collecting.

17 A cavity in a colony of brain coral, probably originally formed around a shellfish, provides an ideal sanctuary for a retiring Blenny.

18-19 Colonies of *Acropora* provide abundant sources of food and refuge to shoals of fish among the forest-like reefs off Papua New Guinea.

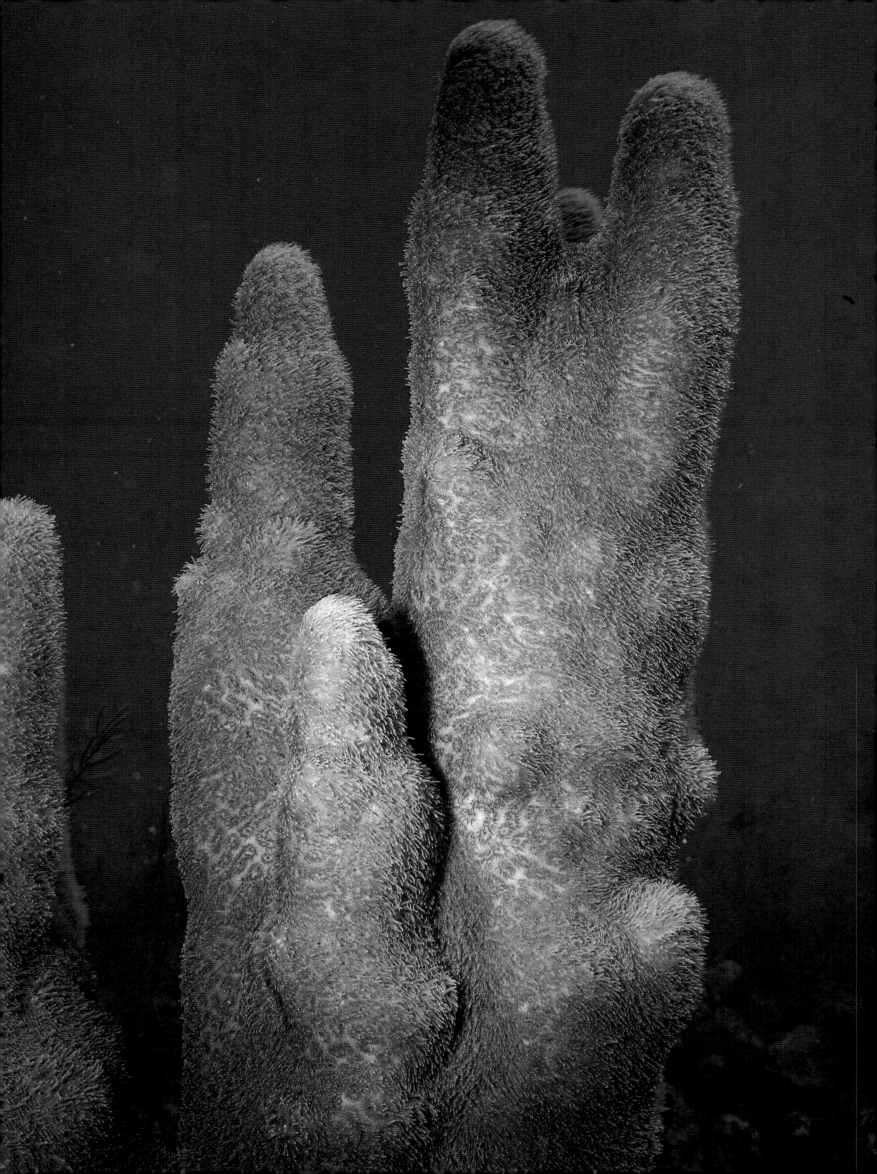

20 These large, vertical, fingerlike growths of pillar coral have probably taken several hundred years to develop to their present imposing state on a Turks and Caicos Reef.

21 A fine example of the large solitary slipper or mushroom coral *(Fungia)* from the Maldive Islands which can reach over eight inches in length.

22-23 Brightly colored corals produce a garden-like aspect in the shallows of the Egyptian Red Sea.

24 An impenetrable stand of elkhorn coral
(Acropora palmata) from a reef off the Turks
and Caicos Islands.

25 Sea whips, sea fans, and soft corals
provide a colorful contribution to a Red Sea
reef.

26 A bubble coral *(Plerogyra)* from the Red Sea, showing the retracted basal spheres containing symbiotic algae. These algae provide an additional food source for the coral.

27 This fire coral *(Millipora sp.)*, with its extended polyps, is not a true coral but a hydroid. It secretes a calcareous coral-like skeleton which is used for carving and jewellery.

28 A magnified view of the inflated spheres
filled with symbiotic algae which occur during
daylight hours at the base of bubble coral
tentacles. During darkness these are deflated.

29 A group of green *Didemnum molle*
contrast markedly against the reef building
corals of the Royal Charlotte Shoal in the
South China Sea.

30-31 A shoal of orange sea perch contrast
with the greens and purples of the Red Sea
coral reefs below them.

32 A shallow water reef at Tarmugli in the
Andaman Islands consists mainly of the plate
coral, *Acropora.* This forms the largest genus
of stony reef-building corals with about one
hundred species.

33 The brain coral from the Turks and Caicos
Islands gets its common name through its
resemblance to a mammalian brain. The
convoluted appearance is produced by the
dividing polyps remaining joined together.

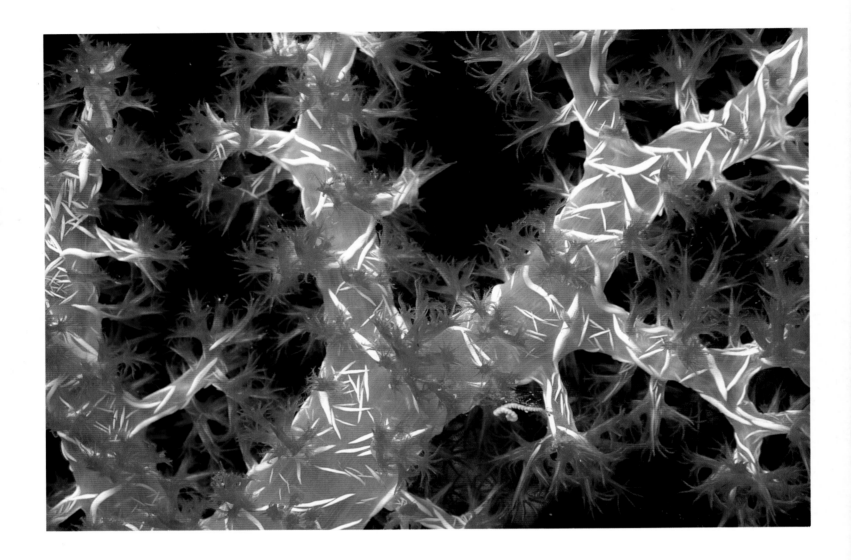

34 These brightly colored alcyonarian polyps take up sea water to provide the branches with rigidity. In the event of adverse currents or storms they expel water and collapse until conditions improve.

35 Shoals of brightly colored fish congregate around the base of a large soft coral which may grow to over six feet in height.

36 A fortunate diver's close up view of the intricate feeding polyps of a brilliant soft coral from the Sipadan reefs off Borneo, Malaysia.

37 Delicate fingerlike tentacles, equipped with stinging cells which immobilize their prey of small fish or invertebrates, sweep the ocean currents in search food.

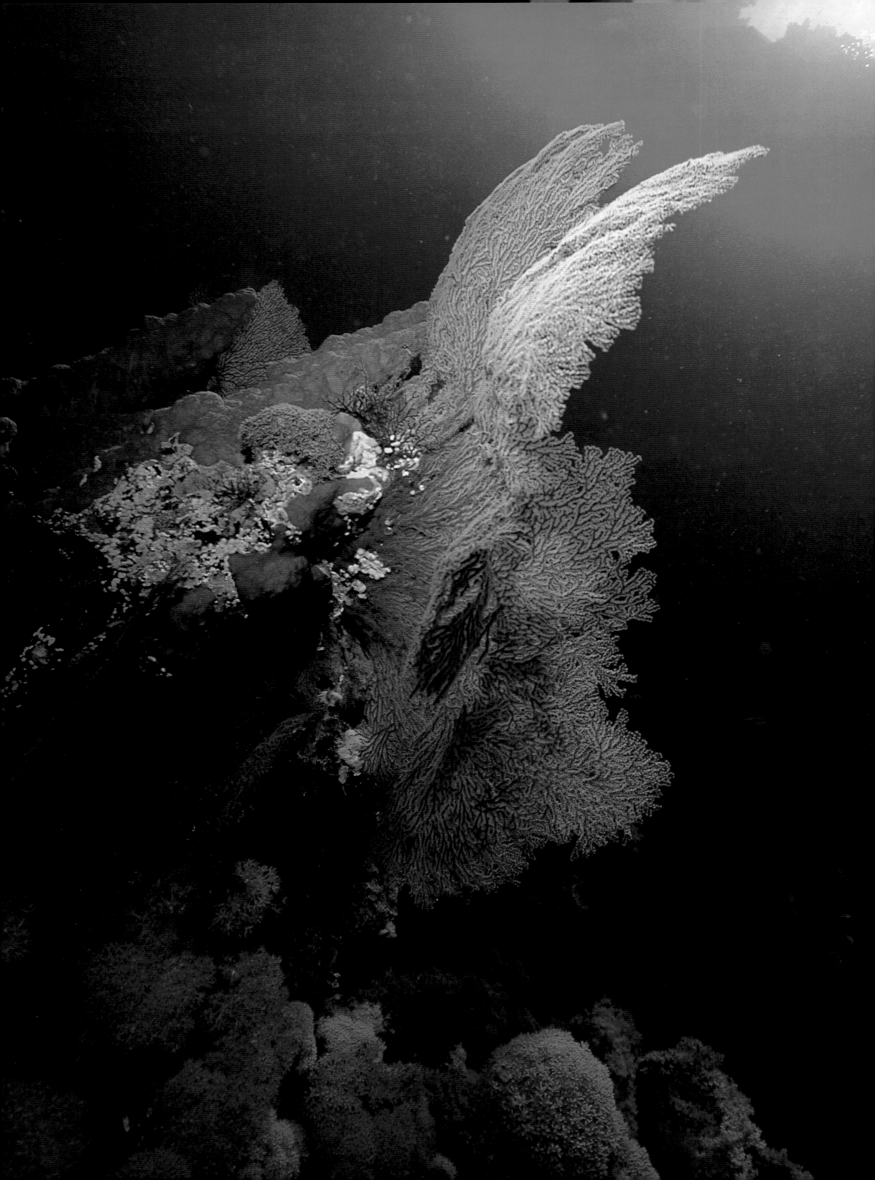

38 A group of sea fans, which may grow up to six feet in height, reflect the comparative tranquility of a sheltered crevice on a Red Sea coral reef.

39 To the uninitiated these brightly colored flowers of the sea appear to be reef dwelling sea anemones but are in fact the feathery food-collecting apparatus of sabellid tube worms.

40 British seas may lack the intricate shapes
of tropical coral reefs but still afford the
beauties of color as shown by these pink and
green jewel anemones off the Devon coast.

41 An exquisitely intricate red sea fan, with its
horny internal skeleton, advertises its
unpalatable nature to other denizens of the
Red Sea through its bright coloration.

42-43 Brightly colored fish swim above large
sea anemones on a coral reef in the Maldive
Islands.

44 A large cup sponge encircles tips of coral
on a Turks and Caicos Islands reef. It is now
believed that sponges help bind coral
fragments together to make the reef more
stable.

45 A diver studies a large anemone with its
associated clown fish searching for scraps
dropped by his companion to the reef below.

LIFE ON THE REEF

Coral reefs constitute perhaps the most prolific of all marine ecosystems, providing an endless variety of niches suitable for exploitation by countless numbers of animals and plants. It is estimated that about a third of all known species of fish are found living among coral reefs which provide them, either directly or indirectly, with a source of food, refuge, or place of safety in which to breed and raise offspring.

Corals themselves, with their stony calcareous skeletons, form the bulk of the reef framework, and colonies of the branching stag's horn coral, or *Acropora*, may make up about 75 percent of the reef in some areas, the numerous branches producing a forest-like effect. This loose lattice, besides providing a source of food for coral-eating fish, also provides ample nooks and crannies in which reef-dwelling fish, sea urchins, starfish, crabs, and shellfish can live in comparative safety. Occasionally, however, this structure can be deadly. Permanent reef dwellers, such as crabs or molluscs, often secrete themselves in the crevices and become entrapped as the coral grows across their means of escape.

Among the more impressive creatures that inhabit the reef are the large giant clams, or *Tridacna*. Their large shell valves, which measure up to four feet across and may weigh over 500 pounds, become embedded in the coral with their gaping aperture exposed to the light allowing single-celled plants to grow in the mantle tissues. The giant clam, in turn, feeds upon these plants.

Life on the reef exhibits seasonal variation since deep-water fish, turtles, and invertebrates migrate to the shallower reef areas to breed. This may be for shelter during this crucial period in the animal's life cycle or for the abundant food supply necessary for its offspring. Similarly, permanent reef dwellers also occur during different periods of the day or night in much the same way as land animals.

The usefulness of coral in supporting life is not merely confined to living reefs. Pieces of living or dead coral are readily detached from the reef by strong currents and cast upon the shore. Here the calcareous skeletons soon become bleached white by the tropical sun, and the resultant coral debris, together with organic material from seaweed and dead animals, forms a basic soil upon which waterborne seeds can germinate. In this way typical coral islands with their coconut palms develop. These are then colonized by seabirds and turtles which in turn also frequent the reef in search of food and nesting materials.

Through the ongoing cycle of regeneration, the coral reef is able to support an amazing variety of organisms. As a precious source of biodiversity it is second to none.

47 Encrusting sponges, corals, and sea fans
mark the junction of an outer reef edge with a
perpendicular cliff face in the Turks and
Caicos Islands.

48 This sea cucumber belongs to the same
group as starfish, featherstars, and sea
urchins. In some areas related species are
actively collected and dried to produce beche-
de-mer.

49 A brightly colored fish seeks a safe haven
at the base of a large Red Sea cup sponge.

50 This barrel sponge from Flores, Indonesia, belongs to the simplest of multicellular animals. It has no muscles or nerves but is ideally adapted to circulate water through its body cavity to capture suspended food particles.

51 A snowflake murray eel bars the progress of a diver off Oman. Secreted among coral crevices by day, murray eels normally emerge at night in search of prey.

52 Two vibrant blue-cheeked butterfly fish
swim nonchalantly over a Red Sea coral reef
apparently unconcerned with a diver's
intrusion into their undersea paradise.

53 A pair of cuttlefish, relatives of the octopus
and squid, swim casually in search of small
fish among the corals of Ari Atoll in the
Maldive Islands.

54 An oriental sweetlips receives welcome attention from a cleaner wrasse among the coral reefs of Ari Atoll in the Maldive Islands.

55 The beautiful form and color of this lionfish, as it swims innocently on its way, conceal its predatory nature and the highly poisonous spines which form its fins.

56

56 This stonefish, a large, bottom-dwelling, predatory relative of the angler fish, merges into its background to lie in wait for its unsuspecting prey.

57 This solitary grouper is carnivorous, and may occupy the same coral crevice for years.

58 A triggerfish swims above Ari Atoll Reef in
the Maldive Islands in search of suitable coral
on which to feed.

59 A squirrel fish swims among the beauties
of a coral garden, with its hard and encrusted
corals, sponges, and algae, while the
foreground is dominated by a large treelike
alyconarian soft coral.

60 A group of featherstars contrast with the
orange sea fan on which they have settled in
the South China Sea.

61 An orange starfish crawls over a cluster of
flask-shaped sponges at Ari Atoll. Water
enters the sponge through the small holes and
is expelled through the large apical hole.

62 This Maldive Islands *Fromia* starfish is a carnivore which feeds on molluscs and other small animals living on the coral reef.

63 This underside view of a cushion starfish shows the five arm rays characteristic of echinoderms, the group to which starfish, featherstars, sea urchins, and sea cucumbers belong.

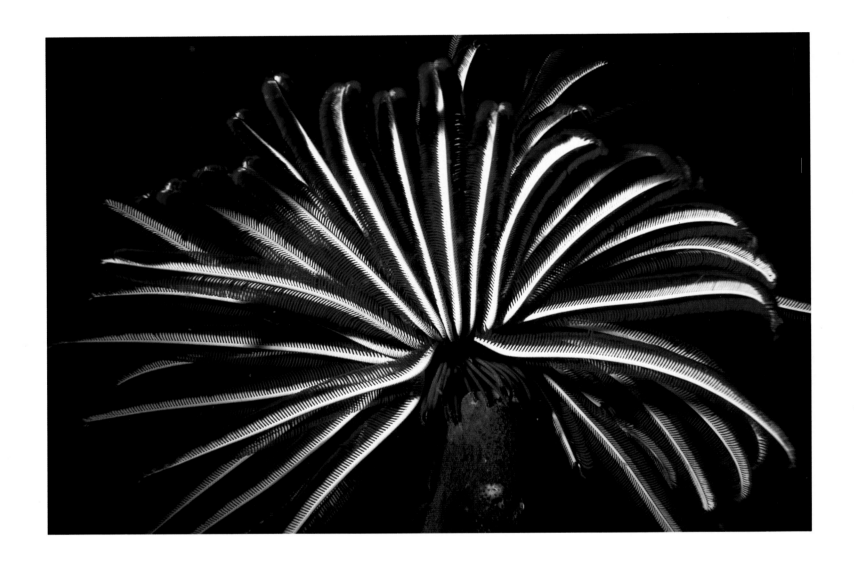

64 This attractive featherstar, a modern relation of crinoids or sea lillies, waves its feathery arms to capture food from the waters of a reef at Ko Dokmal, Phuket, Thailand.

65 A relative of mussels and snails, this exquisitely colored sea slug, *Chromodoris bullocki*, from Borneo, is avoided by predators since they know it is poisonous.

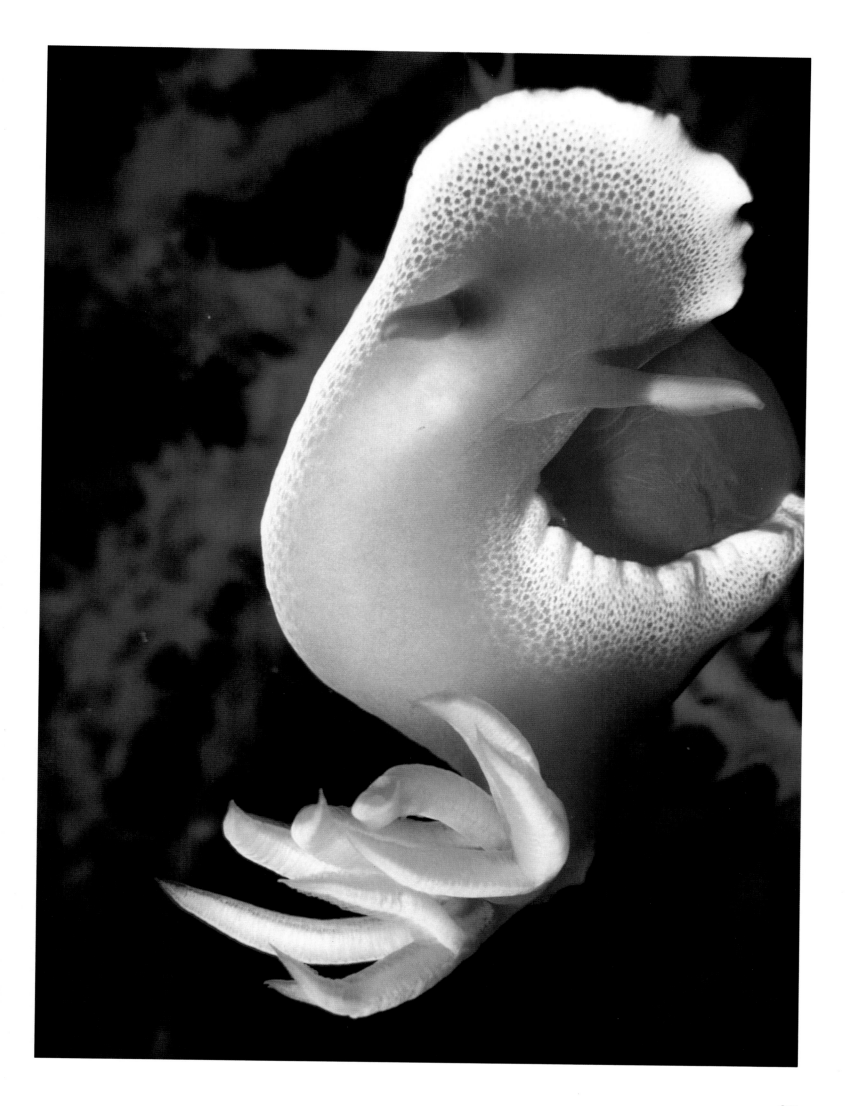

66 Two brightly colored but unpalatable
nudibranches, or sea slugs, crawl over a red
sponge upon which they are most probably
feeding.

67 The tough skinned sea slug *Phyllidia*,
whose mucus secretions prove highly toxic to
predatory fish and may even kill them.

68 Face to face with a green turtle, which
spends most of its life at sea but returns to the
coral island shores to lay its eggs, a process
which normally takes place at night.

69 A green turtle relaxes in the security of a
Red Sea coral grotto, whose inhabitants
provide an abundant source of food.

70 The fleshy mantle lobes of a giant clam
(Tridacna) protrude from between the valves
of their large shell, which is deeply embedded
in the surrounding coral.

71 This New Guinea porcelain crab acts as a
scavenger on the reef. It gets its name due to
the habit of casting off its legs when
threatened.

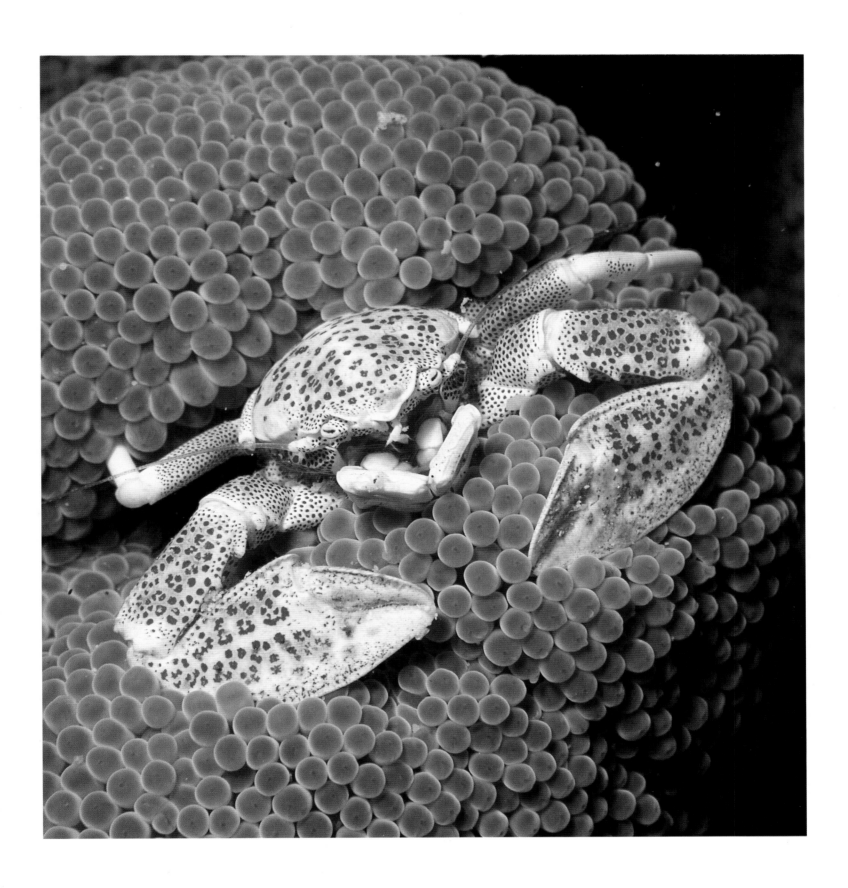

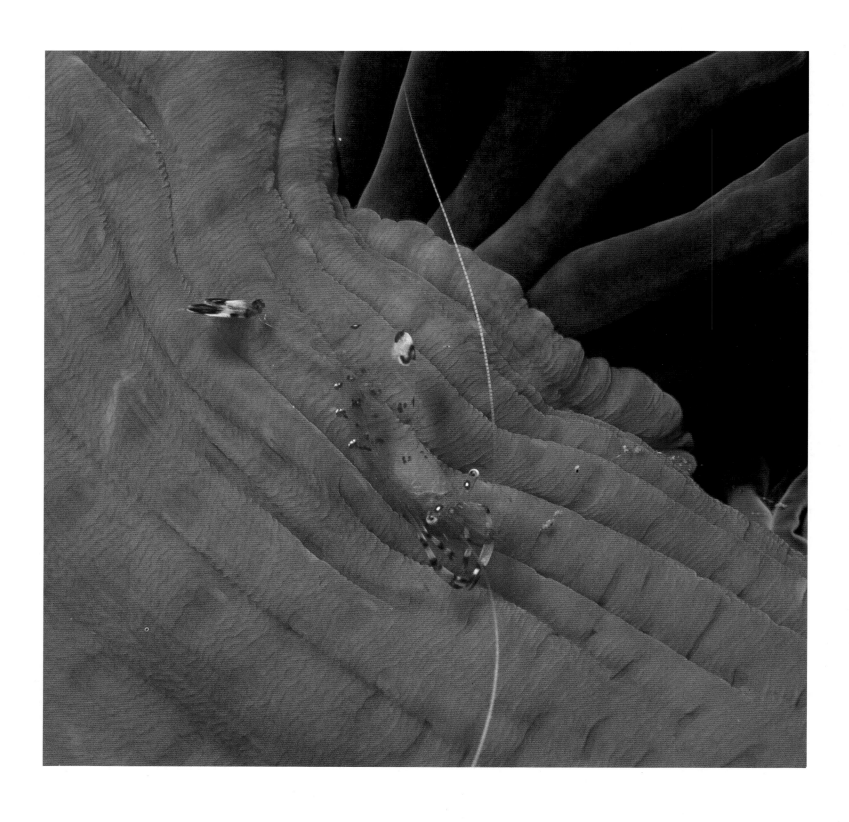

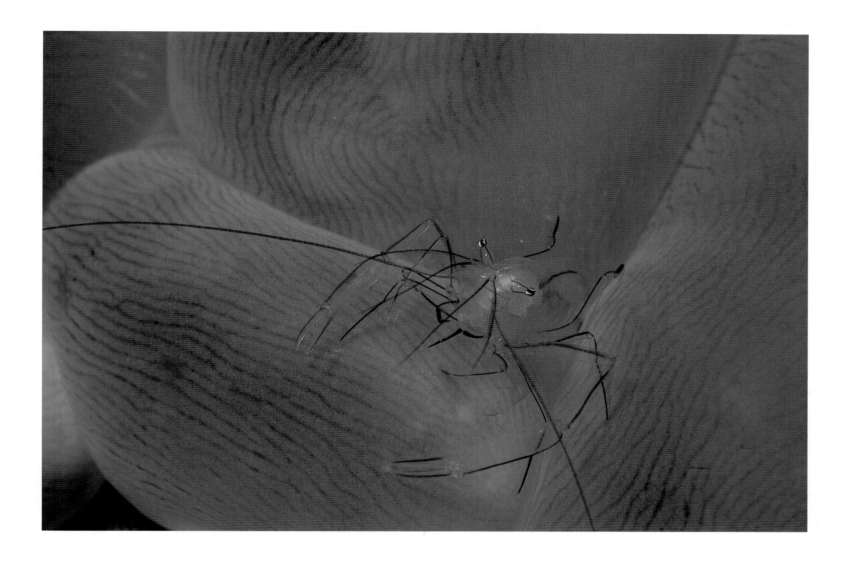

72 Shrimps of the genus *Periclimenes* live
commensally with corals, sea anemones, and
starfish. This example is virtually invisible
against the sea anemone on which it lives.

73 This Indonesian example of the shrimp
Periclimenes occurs on the bubble coral
Plerogyra, its semi-transparent body making it
difficult to find.

74-75 A shoal of dark-banded fusiliers swim
above the coral reefs of Felidu Atoll in the
Maldive Islands.

76 A New Guinea clownfish seeks refuge among the stinging tentacles of a large sea anemone.

77 Many fish species shoal in large numbers, their co-ordinated schooling providing a difficult target for their predators.

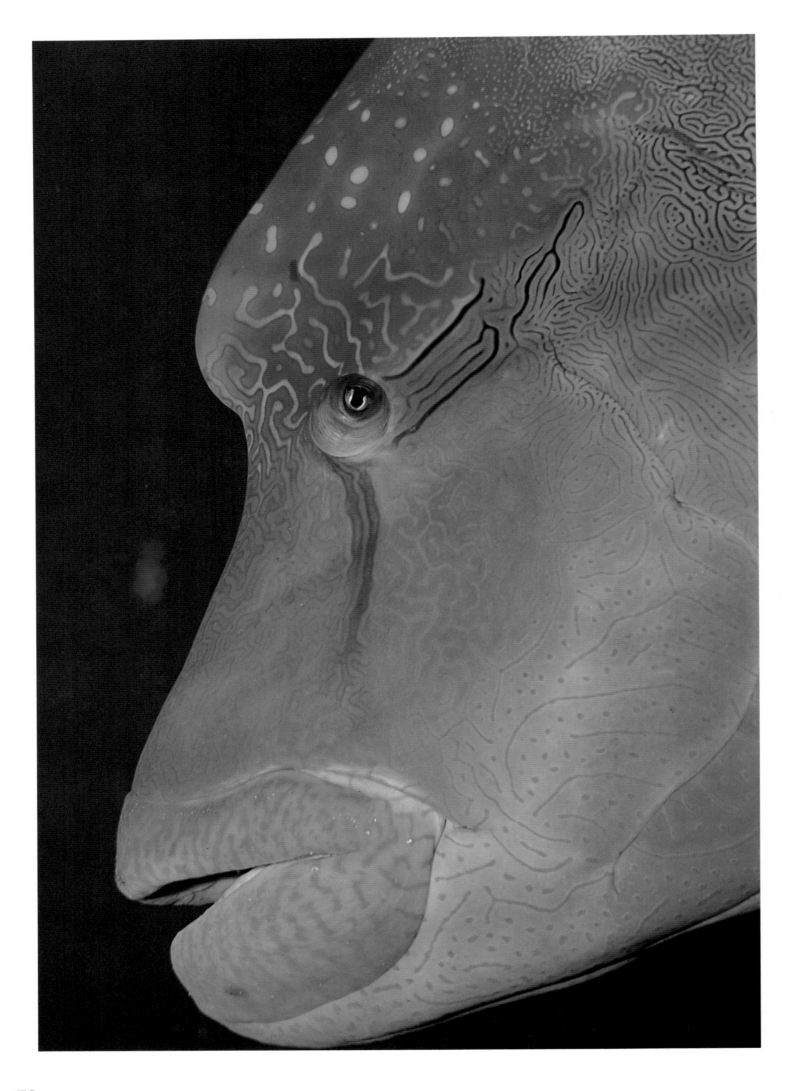

78 The beak-like jaws of this Napoleon
wrasse are well adapted for browsing among
the coral reefs.

79 An exceedingly beautiful *Pyrgoplites
diacanthus* swims gracefully above a coral reef
in the Maldive Islands.

80-81 Shoals of iridescent fish swim like
countless jewels above a coral reef at Flores,
Indonesia.

CORAL REEFS AND MAN

In the past, coral reefs provided a readily available source of food and materials for exploitation by local island communities. The traditional methods employed for catching fish, extracting coral for building, collecting sea cucumbers for "beche-de-mer," and obtaining shellfish for food or as a source of natural pearls were the culmination of centuries of experience of native island communities living in harmony with nature. They ensured a sustainable process with minimal adverse effects upon the coral reefs.

As mentioned, coral reefs represent perhaps the richest marine habitat on earth with about a third of all known species of fish living within them. To add to these riches, mangrove forests develop along the coastal shorelines and colonize the reef flats, the trees being extremely tolerant of the high salt levels and low oxygen content of these coastal waters. The resultant habitat, which is especially rich with crabs, several species of oysters, snails, and fish, considerably increases the food potential for island peoples. In addition, the long ramifying roots help stabilize the muddy deposits and assist in protecting the shoreline from erosion.

The native inhabitants of these Islands, the Micronesians, Melanesians, and Polynesians are expert fishermen who use the sea's resources, together with island birds and turtles, to the full. Being skillful navigators, capable of long voyages in their distinctive canoes, they have become widely distributed throughout the Pacific.

A lack of stone has resulted in the use of shells and coral as building materials. Coral is also used to form tools such as adzes, knives, and hooks, or for drinking vessels, spoons, currency, and adornment.

During the centuries the islanders developed similar harmonious relationships with their surroundings, despite differences in their ancestral cultural traditions. In the case of the Polynesians, property, especially land, belonged equally to everyone with social status, which was dependent on ability. Interestingly, women and the elderly are highly esteemed in their society. Micronesians are skilled navigators, with a distinct class system dependent upon birth and not ability. Unlike other island races, they are noted for producing pottery and woven textiles. The Melanesians are a more male-dominated society, status being based on wealth coupled with powers of leadership and political skill.

The inter-relationship between humans and the reef remained unbroken from man's first appearance in these regions until Cook's voyages in the late eighteenth century. However, the ever-increasing contact with Western civilization has unfortunately upset this natural balance.

83 A Maldive fisherman proudly displays his catch from the North Male Atoll.

84-85 Maldive islanders collecting coral for the local lime kilns.

86 A local fisherman from the Turks and Caicos Islands displays his recent capture from the offshore reef.

87 This captured berried lobster from Ndaveli, Pigeon Island, Sri Lanka, is destined for the dinner table.

88 A local fisherman, with his characteristic
fishing boat, a perahu, prepares to set sail,
near Sabah, Malaysia.

89 Natural stone is scarce on many coral
islands resulting in the use of coral for
buildings and walls, as shown in this example
in the Maldive Islands.

90 Waterborne seeds of mangrove trees
rapidly develop along the shoreline of coral
islands, with their roots immersed in seawater.
They stabilize the substrate as well as trapping
silt in suspension.

91 A native islander cleaning queen conch
shells in the Bahamas, the shells will later be
sold and the meat used for Conch Salad.

92-93 Aerial roots of coastal mangroves
which protrude above the water's surface to
obtain oxygen for the immersed sections.
They also help to consolidated the shoreline.

94 Drying sea-cucumbers for beche-de-mer
at Kota Kinabalu, Sabah, Malaysia.

95 Air-drying fish on board a fishing boat, *La Libertad*, in El Salvador.

96-97 A local shell stall with queen conch
shells, corals, and dried starfish for sale in the
Bahamas.

INTO THE FUTURE

Coral reefs constitute one of the most threatened of marine habitats. Due to their slow growth and relatively long life expectancy, they cannot easily regenerate themselves, and their plight is made even more difficult by the fact that they are permanently cemented to the sea-floor. Hence, increasing pollution and sporadic invasion by predators, such as the crown of thorns starfish, prove particularly devastating.

Through our indiscriminate plunder of marine resources, shallow- and surface-water fish stocks have been greatly reduced – many to virtual extinction. This has resulted in commercial fisheries turning their attention to deep-water species in increasing numbers. One effect of this has been the depletion of some North Atlantic *Lophelia* colonies as a direct result of entanglement in fishnets during deep-sea trawls.

Thus a coral colony which, together with its associated flora and fauna, may have developed over 300 or 400 years, can be wiped out in a matter of minutes. Perhaps even more tragic is the damage done to well-established reefs, such as the Great Barrier Reef of Australia, as many of these reefs have taken over 10,000 years to develop to their present state.

Improved communications and transport add to the problem through increased tourism, the development of coastal resorts, and the erection of airports and harbors. In the past such projects took place without consideration for their effect upon the environment, often resulting in the destruction of the very features of natural beauty which formed the initial attraction of the area.

Further hazards, in the form of pollutants, refuse, sewage, oil, or other toxic substances, released intentionally or through shipwreck, have compounded the problem. Even the methods used in attempting to rectify these catastrophes have sometimes magnified the damage.

Concern for the safety of coral reefs is rising, however, and this concern has resulted in international cooperation to develop codes of conduct for maritime vessels. It has also led to the coordination of research on the effects of man's activities on coral reefs and coastal environments, and to the creation of protected marine areas. These areas can act as replenishment reservoirs for fisheries and are designed to include maximum ecosystem diversity.

It is to be hoped that this initial response for regulating the harvest of marine resources to a sustainable level can satisfy all users of the waters concerned, and that the development of breeding and regeneration programs heralds the first step toward restoring degraded coral reefs to their former glory.

99 A discarded anchor provides a suitable substrate upon which coral and other marine organisms can grow. Sadly most of man's refuse proves less beneficial to the marine environment.

100-101 A mixed shoal of colorful fish swim over a coral encrusted wheel and axle in the Red Sea.

102 Coral-filled cages provide a foundation for a sewer pipe outlet in the Maldive Islands, Indian Ocean.

103 A general view of an exposed reef flat at low tide in the Maldive Islands.

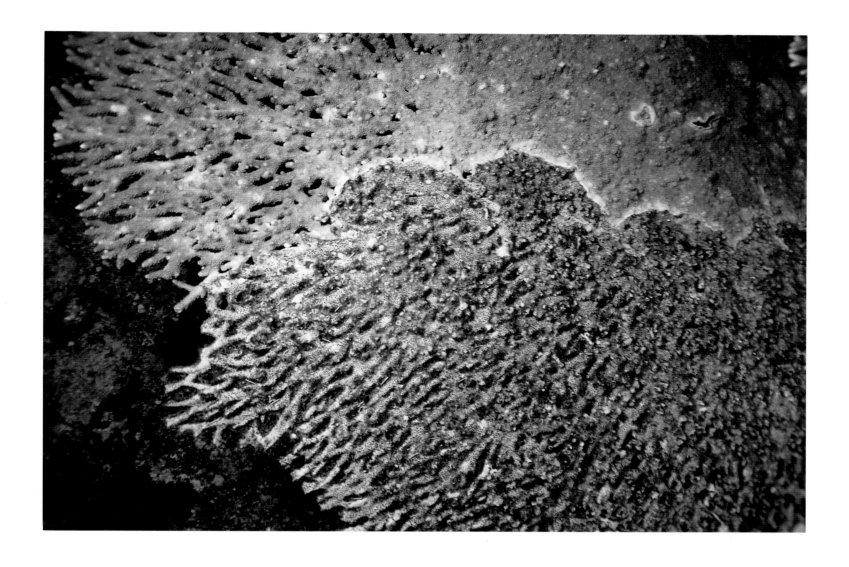

104-105 Man's use of coral is often extensive. Here, coral from a local reef has been used to construct a jetty in the Maldive Islands.

106 An empty tin can nestles among dead coral covered in silt on a reef in the Maldive Islands.

107 A colony of the branching coral, *Acropora*, from the Andaman Islands, showing a healthy, living, green portion and the contrasting gray and white skeletons of a dead area.

108 A dead coral colony covered by a suffocating deposit of silt and algae.

109 *Plerogyra sinuosa* showing live polyps with their symbiotic green algae as well as bleached and dead portions indicating the unhealthy state of this coral colony.

110 A Red Sea example of the crown of
thorns starfish, which is a predator of coral. In
some years these starfish occur in immense
numbers devouring entire coral colonies so
that large areas of reef are killed outright.

111 A close up view of the feet of a crown of
thorns starfish from Fiji in the Pacific Ocean.

112-113 An aerial view of Arlington Reef,
Northern Queensland, which forms part of the
Australian Great Barrier Reef Marine Reserve.

114-115 This aerial view of the southern tip of
Raiatea Island in the Society Islands, shows its
coastal lagoon separating the outer coral reef
from the shore.

116 An aerial view showing the adverse
effects of man-made enclosures in the
Seychelles on mangrove and coastal habitats.

117 A clown fish hides in a large anemone in
the Red Sea. Due to the increased interest in
tropical fish, attractive species such as this are
under threat from intensive collection for
dealers.

118-119 These Indian Ocean coral islands are
part of the Seychelles. An idea of the variation
in water depths can be seen in the lagoonal
area separating the two islands.

120 A tourist's view of the wonders of the Australian Great Barrier Reef through the window of a submersible.

121 Tourists on board a boat excursion to the coral reefs at Hurghada in the Red Sea.

122-123 High school students carrying out original research during a week's field study course on the Great Barrier Reef at Heron Island, Australia.

120

124-125 A subaqua diver explores the underwater mysteries of the Florida Keys.

126 Australia's Great Barrier Reef is revealed at low tide on Green Island.

127 This aerial view of Masthead Island, Australia, shows its surrounding expanse of reef flat.

128 A gray angelfish searches for food among the coral reefs of Grand Turk Island, one of the Turk and Caicos Islands.